C000002566

Take Me
to the Edge

Take Me
to the Edge

Katya Boirand

with photographs by
Eli Sverlander

unbound

Unbound

6th Floor Mutual House, 70 Conduit Street, London W1S 2GF

www.unbound.com

Text design by Lindsay Nash

A CIP record for this book is available from the British Library

ISBN 978-1-78352-713-7 (hardback)
ISBN 978-1-78352-714-4 (ebook)

Printed in China by 1010 Printing International Ltd.

1 3 5 7 9 8 6 4 2

With special thanks to Omar Naeem for his generous support

With grateful thanks also to Darren Cohen, Josh Gilinski, Jason Mcnab, Jeffrey Meyers, Paul Rodgers and Stef Youakim for their support of this book

Introduction

Buried in the bottom of a box, under piles of journals, I found my travel diaries. In amongst my scribblings during a twelve-day Atlantic crossing over eight years ago, the idea to be inspired by somebody's choice of words was born. The seed had been planted for 'Poetry by Me, Inspired by You'.

This project and the creation of this book have been almost enlightening with regards to the choice of words my inspirers have given me. The words will undoubtedly say something about the individual, but what is fascinating is that everyone has commented that the poems I put together appear to hold a message for them.

Each poem is written at speed, often taking no longer than five minutes to write; as I enter the state of flow, it is as if the words are coming through me onto the paper.

I have thoroughly enjoyed meeting so many people from different walks of life and being able to connect with them through the art of poetry. I have not only been writing for people here in London: word selections have been sent to me via social media from all over the world. I have written for people in India, Indonesia, the United States of America, all over Europe, China, Africa, South America and Canada. The word choices from all over each of the continents are so reflective of how connected we really are and how, in spite of our different cultures, beliefs and birthplaces, energy and love always speak the loudest.

The twenty-nine amazing souls that have been included in this book are all very dear to me for so many reasons. They have all touched my life in some way and I am so grateful to have worked alongside them in this chain of creation. With each poem is a photograph illustrating the poetic world, and it all stems from the subject's five chosen words. Their initial idea and spontaneous choice have seen an evolution.

I hope you enjoy this selection of stories told through words and images collected on my adventures across the globe. If you would like a poem of your own written, please don't hesitate in submitting your five words via Instagram to @poetrybymeinspiredbyyou and you may well be featured in the next book.

Katya Boirand, 2018

Poems and Portraits

Andrea Ornstein

MEATPACKING DISTRICT,
MANHATTAN, NEW YORK CITY

+ p.62

A nugget of wisdom

Food for thought

She'll leave her mark on all

Sparkling spirits

Ocean depths

A beauty to enthral.

Gary Lippman

MET MUSEUM, MANHATTAN,
NEW YORK CITY

+ p.62

Eyes fall shut

A warm vermilion

Sleeper slides in

Deeper still

Life's movie plays

The dream does glisten

Restores a calm

One rests until

Kerfuffle strikes

Subconscious enters

Psyche plays a

Devious game

Stand commando

Face the demons

Perfect lustre

Masks the shame.

Andrea Schroeder

TOPANGA CANYON,
LOS ANGELES

+ p.62

Rose-scented memory

Evoked in a beat

Follow your nose

Carry your feet

Spirit is dancing

On life's mortal rhyme

Love can caress through

The senses in time

Freedom so transient

Presented in form

Butterfly bandit

Cooks up a storm.

Jonas Myrin

BEECHWOOD CANYON,
LOS ANGELES

+ p.63

Vagabond heart melting so gently
Unwritten melody cushions the yield
Atlas-shaped castle envelops a dreamer
Miracle rising to play golden field.

Naurija Ziukaite

SHOREDITCH, EAST LONDON

+ p.63

My love, my one

I implore you

Take me to the edge

Surrender your heart

Never lose faith

And join me in

A dance beyond

Infinity!

Nikita Andrianova

SHOREDITCH, EAST LONDON   + p.63

Losing fascination

With the glory

Of creation

As intelligence in

Robot form

Is so alive

Becomes the norm

Reality exciting now

Duality our world

Somehow

A beautiful

Reincarnation

Of raw truth is

Love's salvation.

Matt McCabe

WESTMINSTER BRIDGE,
LONDON

+ p.64

Legends and fables
Dream through the night
Dragon inferno
Rise and take flight
Soar across waters
Ripple in time
Fold fear beneath love
Feel peace in its prime.

Magdalena Sverlander

SOUTH KENSINGTON,
LONDON

+ p.64

Loyalty grows
In limitless love
A true dream flows
From a power above.

Kwaku Osei-Afrifa

HYDE PARK, LONDON

+ p.64

Lavender mist rolls

Ardently through

Ethereal scapes

Telescopic mind

Each pointed remark

Ricochets fast

Amorous move

Stripped naked in kind.

Trish Campbell

+ p.65

Phoenix ashes dormant
Drenched in salty tears
Heartache recollecting
Old fragmented fears
Naked with confusion
Try to hide love's rash
Call on earthly angels
To dry the sodden ash.

Portia Van de Braam

NORTH LANES, BRIGHTON   + p.65

In a transient flurry
She'll float on by
Smooth wounded hearts
When souls do cry
Bequeath expertise
In a passion for life
Forage salvation
For those blind in strife.

Max Rodman

NATURAL HISTORY MUSEUM,
LONDON

+ p.65

Throw down the broom

Snuggle her close

Play the love martyr no more

Step into your tweed

The show will commence

Scrumptious man take to the floor!

Imogen Prowse

+ p.66

Walk the blade edge
Swing from the highest branch
Ride the fastest arrow
Drop from the moon
And land among the stars
Never lose hope
You are almost there!

Luc Waring

+ p.66

Society's paradigm
Crumbles beneath us
The gods have spoken
The time has come
Be your own president
Govern your own internal world
Distant family unites to see
A universal soul emerge.

Alexandra Long

WANDSWORTH COMMON,
LONDON

+ p.66

Excuse me while

I intercede on

Behalf of the universe

To call upon a

New friend

A magical woman

In diaphanous white

Oozing sex appeal

And joy

Protect your heart

But always be

Overexposed in

Your art!

Abigail Johns

CLAPHAM,
SOUTH LONDON

+ p.67

Melting honey-laden wax into

A smouldered candle rising

Striking many matches

A charcoal-fingered burden

Flame denied full access

A knight of tempting flickers

Penetrator closer

Insouciance last curtain.

Luke Portman

MARYLEBONE, LONDON + p.67

A simple hello
To diffuse any tension
Dark night of the soul
Disappears
A rose drops her thorns
Internal ascension
A creak of divine
Negates fear.

Ian Cameron

OXFORD CIRCUS, LONDON

+ p.67

Rein in your addiction
Surrender your heart
Control is your weapon
And choice is your art
Expansion emerges...

Rosalind Noctor

LEWISHAM, LONDON

+ p.68

Glide euphoric

Gently through

A dance of atoms

Born anew

As ego drops

Its petalled flower

Life organic

Grows in power

Touch expansive

Realms sō true

So orgasmic

Beautiful you.

Hazel Thompson

LEWISHAM, LONDON   + p.68

Dragonfly speed
Nimble and pure
Cut diamond eyes
Reflecting the cure
Hope for a compass
To guide and incite
Map of her world
Encoded with light.

Ed Voyce

CLAPHAM JUNCTION,
LONDON

+ p.68

Existential salt in wound

Sleep through pain of

Days gone by

Raw persistence rips in two

Torn between a

Laugh and cry

Laser-focused purpose

Sets a raging fire

Symbolic birth

Grasping honour in both hands

Maintain a life

So down to earth.

Inga Holth

PRINCE ALBERT BRIDGE,
LONDON

+ p.69

Dance among fairy-lights

Whimsical space

Blur effervescently

Inhuman race

Rise beyond flames

Set fire to your heart

Sphere of vibration

Sparks magic to start.

Lenka Chubuklieva

CLAPHAM JUNCTION,
LONDON

+ p.69

Clandestine fire

Waiting to erupt

The deepest treasure

Just out of reach

Leather laces

Anchor her desire

Until the moment

Breathes and becomes

Experimental

In its entirety.

Angeline Elliott

TOWER BRIDGE, LONDON

+ p.69

A life full of love

My half-blood connection

Adventure is now

Energy injection

Happiness evolving...

David Urban

SHEPHERD'S BUSH, LONDON + p.70

Screaming out conflict

Full steam ahead

Sex without intimacy

That's what she said

Tactile submission

Will penetrate core

Pain ever growing

He comes back for more.

Darren Cohen

CENTRAL LONDON

+ p.70

Capricious being throw that caution

See it caught in windy skies

Gravitas will represent the torpid

Depth behind their eyes

Shine a light on dusty corners

Words escaping from the heart

Play life's game with cool surrender

Taking solace in your art.

Marta Hermida

CLAPHAM, LONDON

+ p.70

Fearless heart
With a whispering
Tenderness
Your determination
Flows through
Body channels
So electric that
A laughing resilience
Grows into an
Ardent adaptability.

Alex Boirand

+ p.71

It's all belief
Said the heart
Add the mindset
Said the head
Determination
Said the spirit
Strength in choice
Abundance said.

Loris Benito

L'ARC DE TRIOMPHE, PARIS   + p.71

Surprise felicity

Born from a

Mesmerising reciprocity

Infinite possibilities unfold

In a warm embrace

Where protection is

Paramount.

The Subjects and Their Words

Andrea Ornstein

Nugget · Food · Ocean · Beauty · Sparkling

An angel, a mother and a beautiful light in a sometimes dark world, Andrea is love personified with an incredible intellect and lust for life. Wherever she goes she will bring out the best in everyone she meets, and I am very lucky to call her a friend.

Gary Lippman

Glisten · Lustre · Kerfuffle · Commando · Vermilion

An incredible writer for the *New York Times* among other publications, Gary can shape many an idea with his tapestry of words. His kindness ripples through the hearts of everyone he meets, and as a solid family man, he travels the world but always returns home to New York.

Andrea Schroeder

Spirit · Butterfly · Freedom · Love · Rose

So open in her vulnerability and so pure of heart, Andrea is a mother, a successful entrepreneur and an all-round incredible woman. Her wonderful, undeniable self-expression was so evident during the photoshoot at her beautiful home in Topanga Canyon, Los Angeles that all involved felt instantly at home.

Jonas Myrin

Vagabond · Atlas · Melody · Dreamer · Miracle

A raw talent, a man of music and a warrior of light, Jonas sees the good in everyone he meets, has an uncanny ability to make you feel alive yet at peace, and blesses the world with pure grace in every single one of his songs.

Naurija Ziukaite

Infinity · Surrender · You · Edge · Never

From Lithuania but now London-based, this politically inclined beauty has a knack for leading people, understanding human nature and inspiring others. She loves freely and adventures endlessly.

Nikita Andrianova

Beautiful · Exciting · Fascination · Alive · Creation

A queen of social media, a beauty and a very busy creative director, Nikita is a softly spoken powerhouse of a woman with a focus and determination that will carry her in any direction she chooses.

Matt McCabe

Dragon · Ripple · Rise · Peace · Beneath

Matt is a truly lovely Irish gentleman with a creative mind and a talent for acting both in theatre and film. He even recited poetry to passers-by as we photographed him on Westminster Bridge, which is basically how he lives his life: with no qualms and giving to others as much as he can.

Magdalena Sverlander

Love · Loyalty · Limitless · Dream · Power

Softly spoken yet strong in character, Maggie is a mother, a charismatic performer and a wonderful friend. Her care for those close to her and beyond is second to none and her sparkling eyes reflect the joy she feels for life.

Kwaku Osei-Afrifa

Amorous · Pointed · Ethereal · Telescopic · Lavender

Kwaku is a man of words, a writer and a large part of why this book exists as he saw the seed and helped to plant it. He has many stories to tell and is only at the beginning of his journey.

Trish Campbell

Love · Confusion · Phoenix · Angel · Fragmented

My mother, a free spirit, a wild woman and a sensitive soul. Trish is a yoga teacher living on the Isle of Wight and has lived many lives within her sixty years. She has and continues to inspire so many people as a teacher and now as an active member of the community!

Portia Van de Braam

Bequeath · Smooth · Forage · Blind · Transient

A creative, a dreamer and an amazing performer, Portia will greet you with her quirky nature and leave you with a profound imprint of a woman of the world. Always smiling and always with a kind word, she is a gem of a woman.

Max Rodman

Broom · Tweed · Martyr · Snuggle · Scrumptious

One of the most fun-loving, open-hearted people I know, Max is all about the people and connections and brings a lot to his communities all over the world, in his work and in his personal life. As a dreamer who takes action, he is a true example of what you can achieve if you put your mind to it.

Imogen Prowse

Branch · Drop · Hope · Arrow · Blade

A gentle soul, a creative, an avid baker and a breath of fresh air, Imogen is a woman who wears her heart on her sleeve, seeks out adventure and gives love to so many. Her smile is always ready and her mind will keep you captivated.

Luc Waring

Soul · Family · Gods · President · Paradigm

Spontaneous, artistic, an explorer and a romantic, Luc is a very talented artist working with a range of techniques yet with his own specific style. He is joyful and approaches life head on, embracing every opportunity.

Alexandra Long

Intercede · Diaphanous · Overexposed · Magical · Sex

Quietly spiritual, Alexandra spends her days as a fashion designer, observing the world, reflecting its beauty and working harmoniously with nature to produce her garments. This warrior woman emanates a fearless heart and a strong sense of self.

Abigail Johns

Insouciance · Knight · Wax · Burden · Penetrator

She may only be in her early twenties, but Abi speaks as if she has lived many lives before. She will disarm you with her profundity and is often philosophical in the most spiritual of ways. Abi is an actress in the making but I have a sense her life could go in any direction she desires.

Luke Portman

Dark · Diffuse · Rose · Hello · Creak

A fascinating character with stories to tell and anecdotes aplenty, Luke is talented in many areas of life so turns his hand when he can. He is a man of London from many generations back yet is as free-spirited as they come.

Ian Cameron

Expansion · Control · Choice · Surrender · Addiction

With humour and a smile, Ian will always bring his A game to every endeavour. He takes what life throws at him and will always mould it into a positive outcome. With his huge talent as an actor, it is exciting to see what will come next.

Rosalind Noctor

Ego · Organic · Expansive · Orgasmic · Euphoric

A childhood friend, a divine soul and a heart with an understanding of the world that is clear yet colourful. A true dancer, a designer of beautiful clothes and a family woman, she is a blessing to anyone lucky enough to have her cross their path.

Hazel Thompson

Diamond · Hope · Incite · Dragonfly · Compass

She has seen the world in all its pain and glory, with her eyes and through a lens. Her photographs tell so many stories and now her writing is speaking her truth as well. Hazel's energy is electric, and I will always look forward to our serendipitous life meetings.

Ed Voyce

Pain · Persistence · Honour · Purpose · Existential

With a mind as quick as lightning, he will thrill you with his knowledge whilst being the most charming of men. As an entrepreneur, Ed is both creative and logical in his approach and will always be there for you with his words of wisdom.

Inga Holth

Fairy-lights · Blur · Fire · Magic · Sphere

An actress from Norway, residing in London, Inga brings her sparkle and magic wherever she goes. With a love of travel, the world and meeting new people, she can be at home anywhere.

Lenka Chubuklieva

Clandestine · Treasure · Fire · Experimental · Leather

With so many strings to her bow, this lady is always on the go. Lenka will always make time for you though, and her infectious energy is second to none. This music manager and fitness queen will always be ready with a hug.

Angeline Elliott

Life · Energy · Adventure · Love · Happiness

A creative traveller who can turn her hand to any new challenge that comes her way and will always move in the direction of adventure. My funny, smart and joyful sister will never fail to make me and all who meet her laugh, but she is also wise beyond her years.

David Urban

Conflict · Sex · Pain · Submission · Intimacy

David is a fastidious yet imaginative writer as well as a keen reporter and documentary film-maker. His work has taken him all over the world and he intends to continue his explorations for years to come.

Darren Cohen

Capricious · Depth · Gravitas · Heart · Shine

A successful entrepreneur, a wordsmith and a man of incredible intellect, Darren is generous and kind to all he meets. He is one for travel and adventure but still the bringer of fun on his home turf in London and is always someone you want around.

Marta Hermida

Tenderness · Resilience · Adaptability · Fearless · Determination

Whimsical and stubborn, strong yet vulnerable, Marta brings all of her colours and more to the stage and film set and beautifully shares her world and experiences in her life as an actress. She may be from Spain but her soul belongs everywhere so who knows where her roots will be laid when this book goes to print.

Alex Boirand

Abundance · Strength · Determination · Belief · Mindset

French-born and now residing on the Isle of Wight, my wonderful brother Alex serves his community, not only with his delicious humour but also as a firefighter. He is too kind for words and brings the world alive with his dancing, jokes and magical energy. It makes me so happy knowing he has found the love of his life, pictured with him.

Loris Benito

Felicity · Infinite · Warm · Protection · Mesmerising

A skilled footballer residing in Switzerland, Loris is young in years but an old soul who has found his place in this world and perfectly balances ambition with humility. His sense of calm and wonder is like none I've ever seen.

Acknowledgements

To everyone who has supported me with this project, either directly or indirectly, I thank you from the bottom of my heart! To all of my pledgers, I could not have done this without you. To everyone who selflessly took the time and energy to come and shoot with me all over the world and share your creative spirit, I am indebted to you. To everyone on my journey through life who inspires me to write and continues to encourage my adventures with words, you give me life. Sometimes we never know what our calling is until other people show us the way!

A Note on the Author

French-born and half English, it was never clear where home was for Katya Boirand. A childhood on the Isle of Wight, dance and performing arts school in Surrey, university in Kent then Paris, and acting school in New York meant that life was always on the move.

Katya finally put down some roots in London in 2013, to put pen to paper as well as mould an acting career. Her writing includes screenwriting, poetry and exploring the world of a diarist. *Take Me to the Edge* is her first collection of poems in print.

A Note on the Photographer

Eli Sverlander is a Swedish photographer based in Paris and Stockholm. She shoots editorials alongside various advertising and commercial projects as well as finding time to pursue her personal artistic endeavours.

Unbound is the world's first crowdfunding publisher, established in 2011.

We believe that wonderful things can happen when you clear a path for people who share a passion. That's why we've built a platform that brings together readers and authors to crowdfund books they believe in – and give fresh ideas that don't fit the traditional mould the chance they deserve.

This book is in your hands because readers made it possible. Everyone who pledged their support is listed below. Join them by visiting unbound.com and supporting a book today.

Abhishek Advanil

Rasmus Andersen

Eileen Armstrong

Camilla Bannebjerg

Adie Barker

Ahmed Bayyari

Reda Benali

Loris Benito

Rupert Berkmann

Diana Biggs

Vincent Bradley

Paul Brennan

Nick Brock

Ursula Brunetti

Marc Jacques Burton

Diego BV

Ruby & Jock Campbell

Trish Campbell

Lindi Campbell Clause

Zade N Chalhoub de Lusignan

Brian Chappon

Rom Chautard

Lenka Chubuklieva

B Cooper

Lu & Ashton Crosby

Dan

Ben Digby

Patrick Drake

Norman Durance

Angeline Elliott

Daniel Elliott

Pete Elliott

Rhona Eskander

Luca Faloni

Hoss Faridany

Margent Farm

Nabil Fattal

Rupert Fawcett

Ali Fikree

Justin Fisher

Antony Genn

Gil Goldberg

Ithai Goldberg

Diana Gomez

Alan Greenspan

Alexander Gromadzki

Cem Gul

Brian Gumbel

Mona Haj

Youssef Hammad

Tyler Harnish

Steven Harris

Andrew Harvey

Martu Her

Tim Hipperson

Lisa Huep

Neil Hutchinson

Peter Huyck

Angus Jack

Will Johnson

Cj Jones

Scott Kennedy

Thomas Keown

Dan Kieran

Catherine Kinsman

Tony Lazaropoulos

Emma Lingard-Lane

Steve Liu

Luca Longobardi

Marie Lupang

Charlie Lycett

Torsten Mack

Maja Malnar

Laurent Manuel

Tommaso Marzotto

Ryan Masiello

Matty McCabe
Jeffrey Meyers
Roger Michael
Danny Minnick
John Mitchinson
Liban Mohamed
Liban Mohammed
Damian Mould
Sean Nammock
Fab Nap
Carlo Navato
Graeme Nicoll
John O'Sullivan
Andrea, Jake & Alma Ornstein
Kwaku Osei-Afrifa
Percy Parker
Antonio Perez
Justin Pollard
Luke Portman
Alessandro Possati
Lauren Powell
Aneel Ranadive
Uberto Rapisardi
Philip Rebeiz
Tiago Reis Marques
Paul Rodgers
Max Rodman

Riccardo Romani
Kim Ross
Riccardo Ruini
Leila Sadeghee
Indoo Sella
Joshua Skurla
Matt Spangler
Thea Sprecher
Matt Stevens
Emma Stokes
Drew Stroud
John-Christian Sullivan
Erin Summe
Joseph Sung
Christopher Taylor
Alex Tepper
Evan Themelakis
David Urban
Portia Van de Braam
Luc Waring
Adam Williams
Noah Wunsch
Arran Yentob
Rob Young